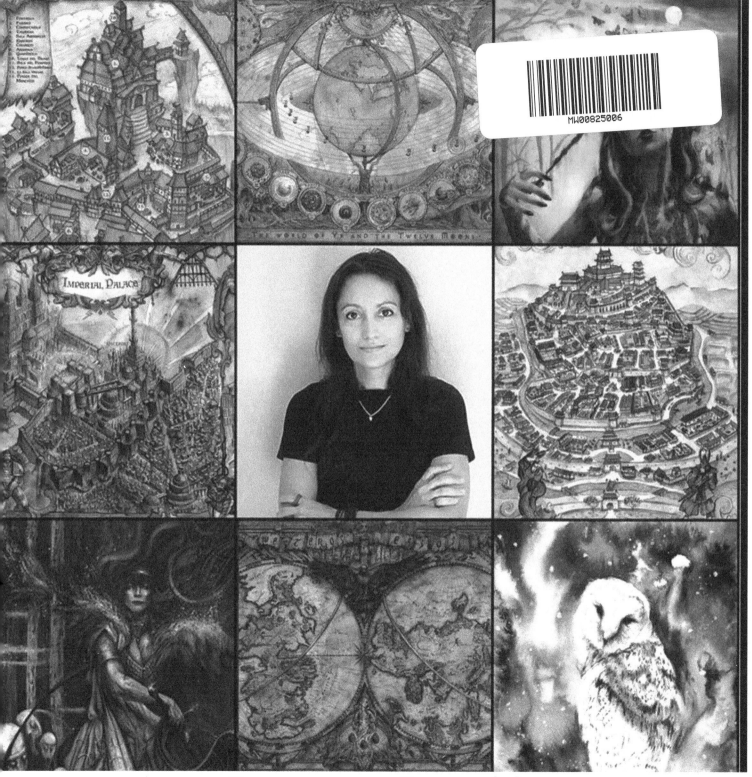

Francesca Baerald

Tsera's Gift Episode 1 The Perfect Tear
Official Coloring Book

Part 1

Thank you to the amazing artist and wonderful person that is Francesca Baerald. Francesca happily took on the task of doing over 150 original watercolors to help support my book even before I had a publisher. Please enjoy her work with your own artistic endeavors and if you would like single sheets to try again with, just email your proof of purchase to info@connielansberg.com and we will send them to you.

To see the original watercolors, please go to @theperfecttear on Instagram.

To join my newsletter, please go to www.connielansberg.com

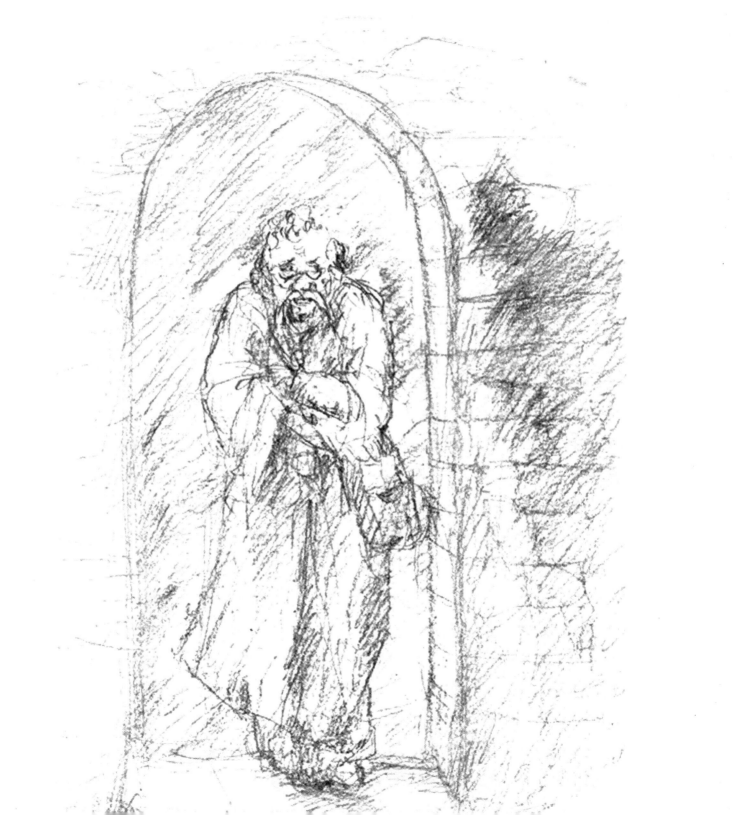

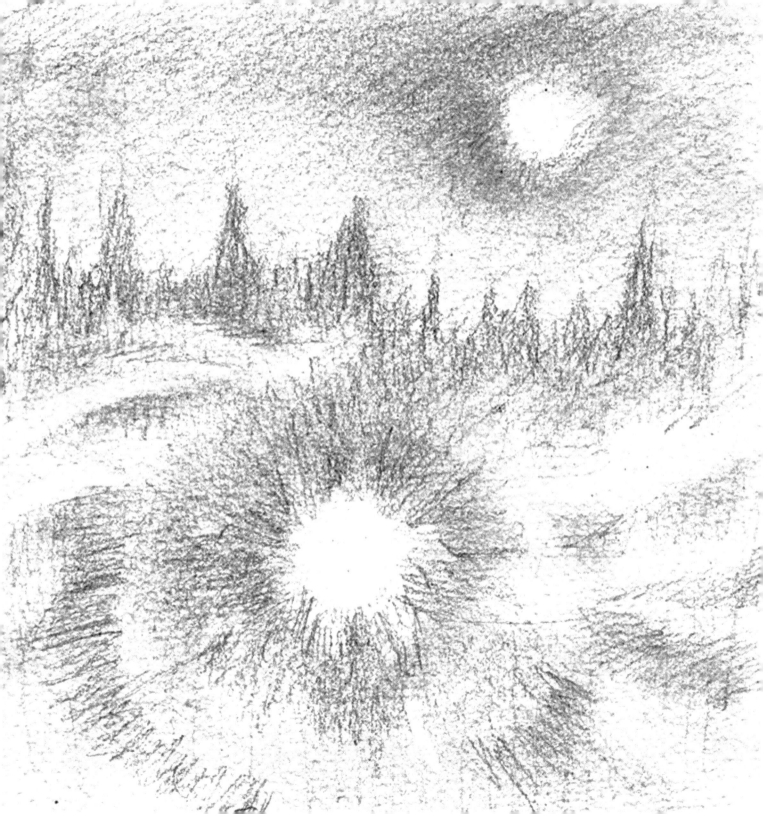

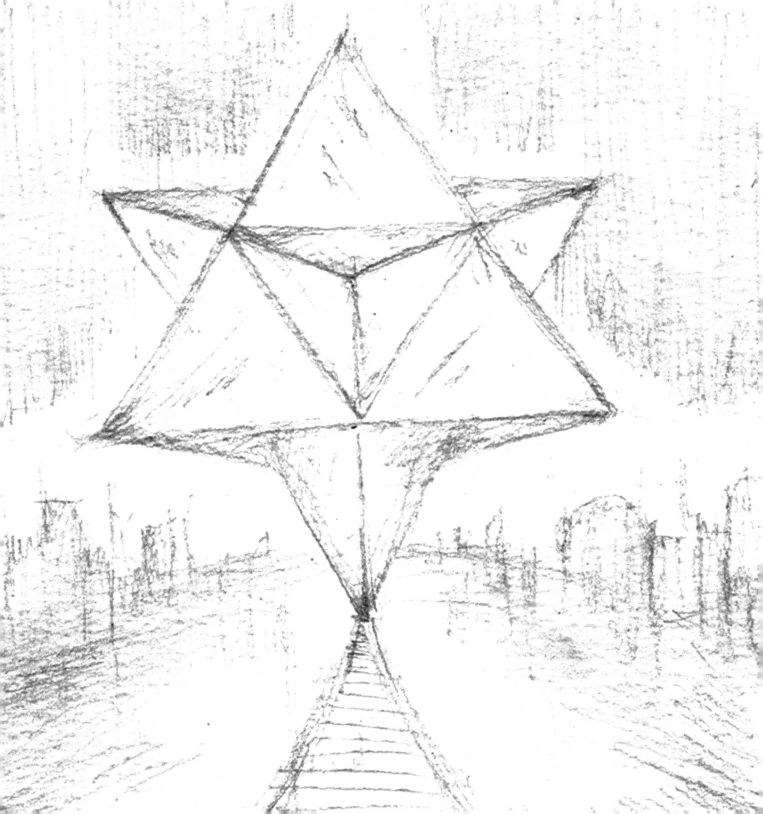

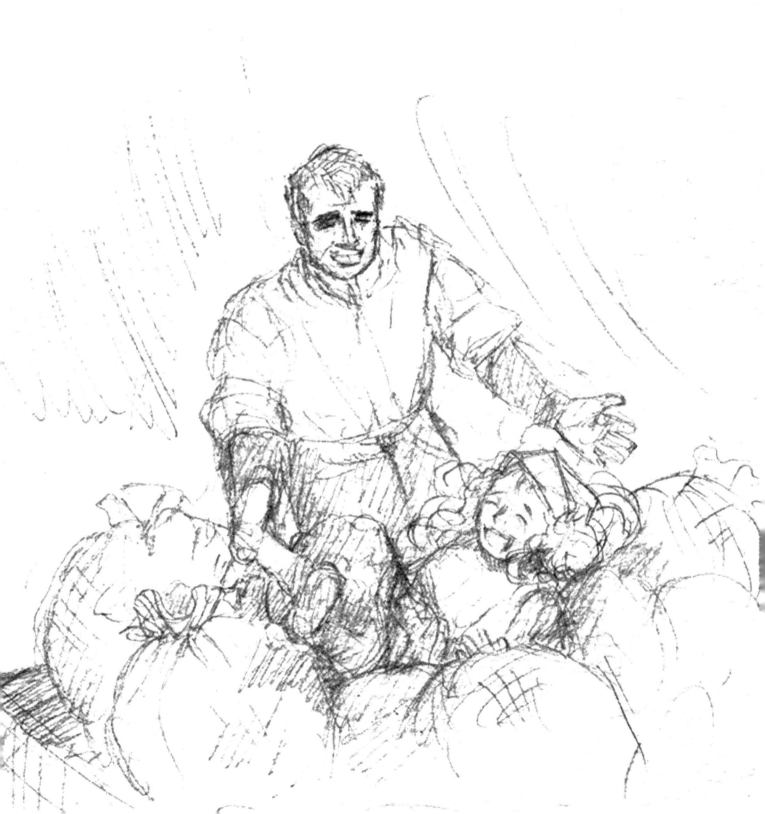

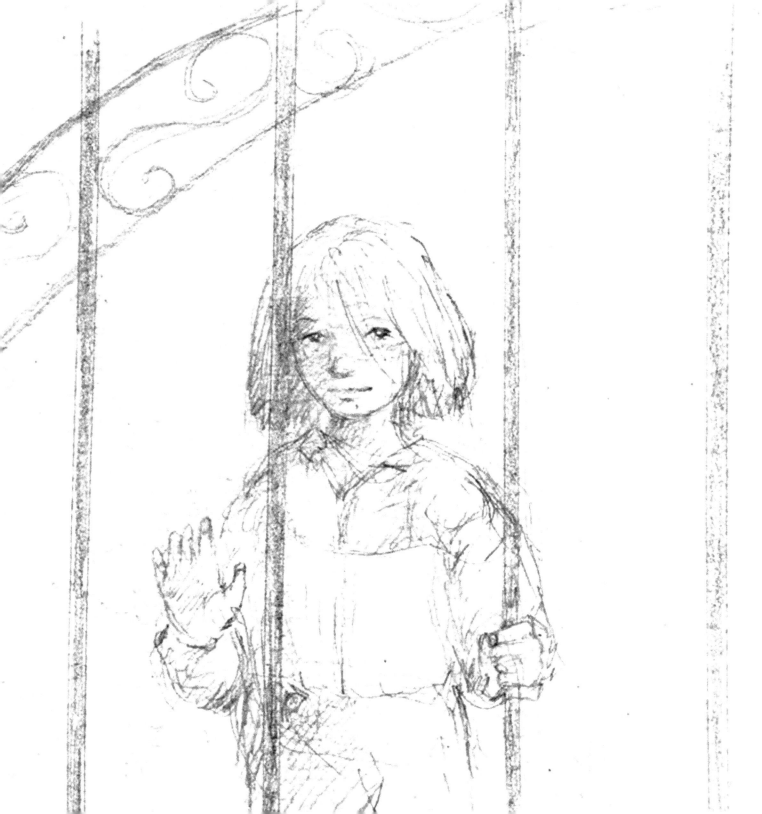

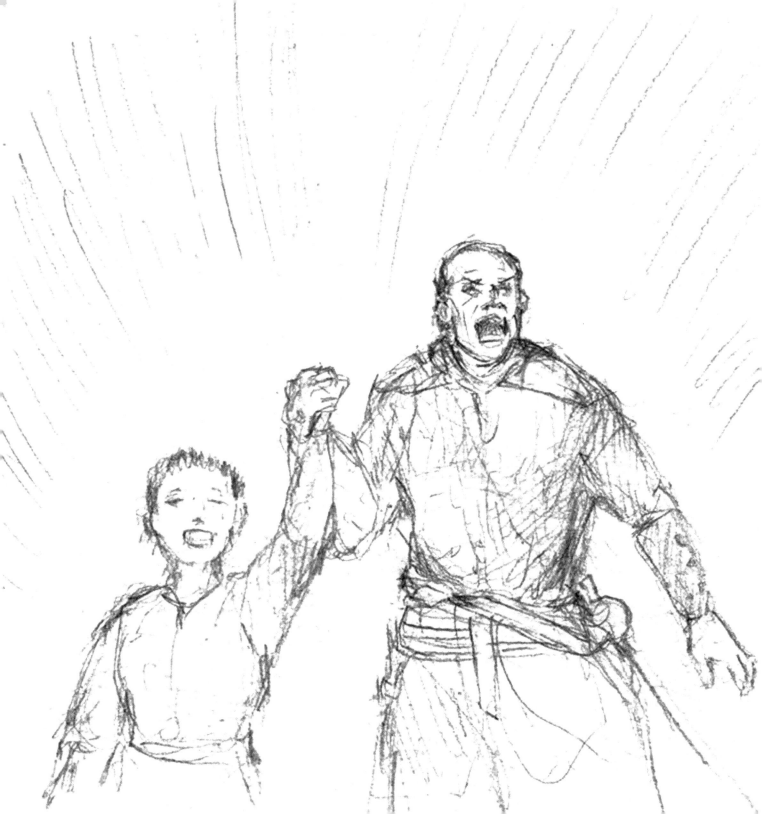

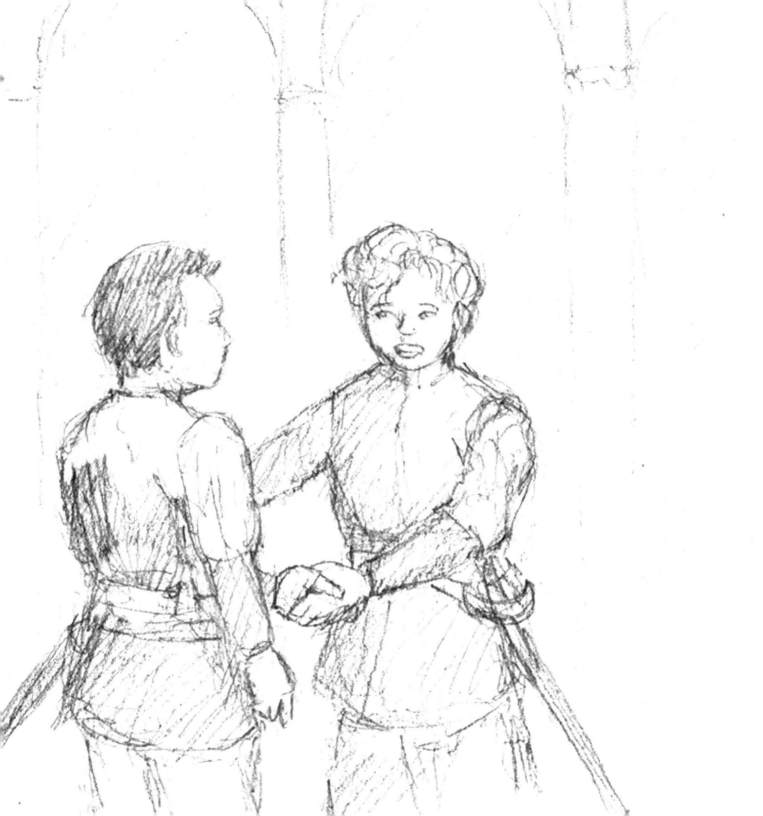

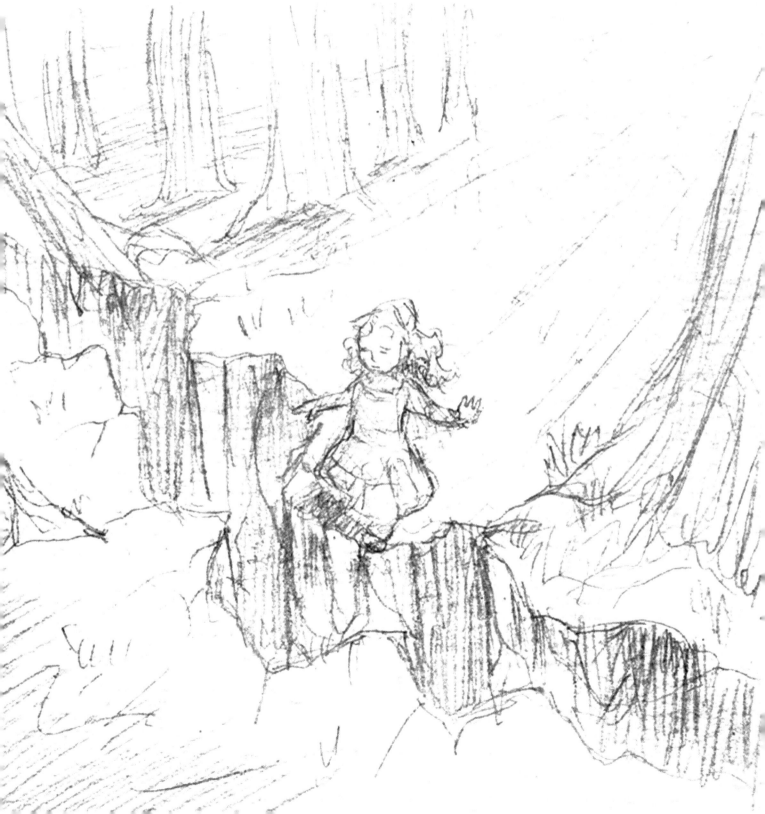

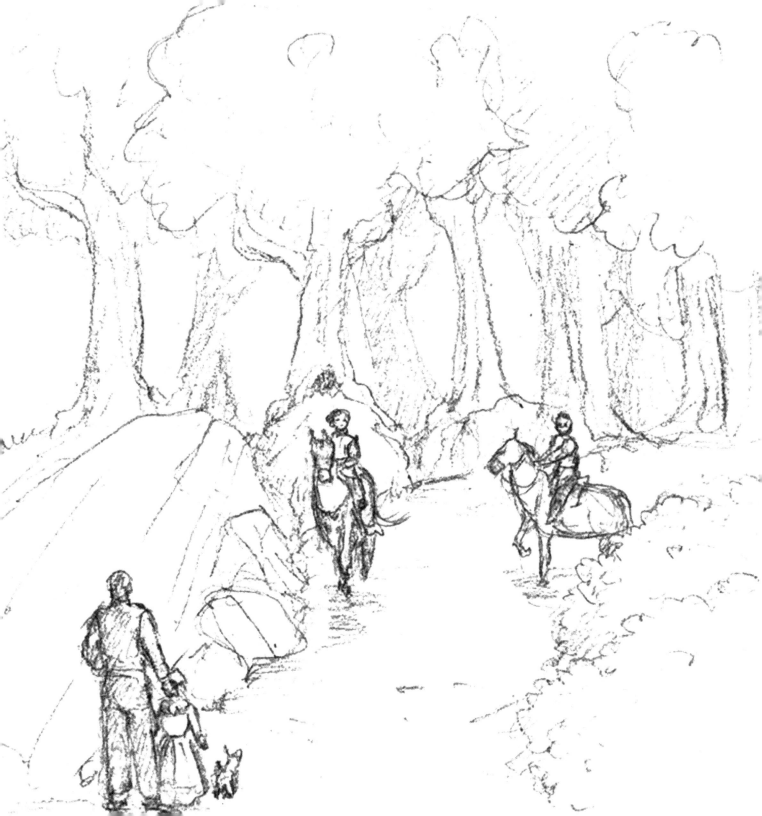

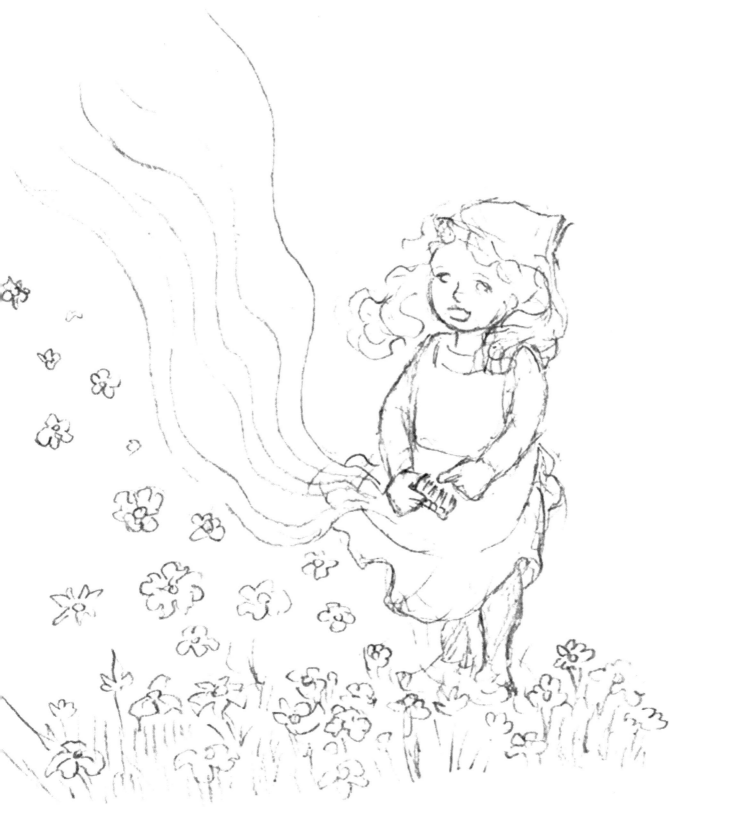

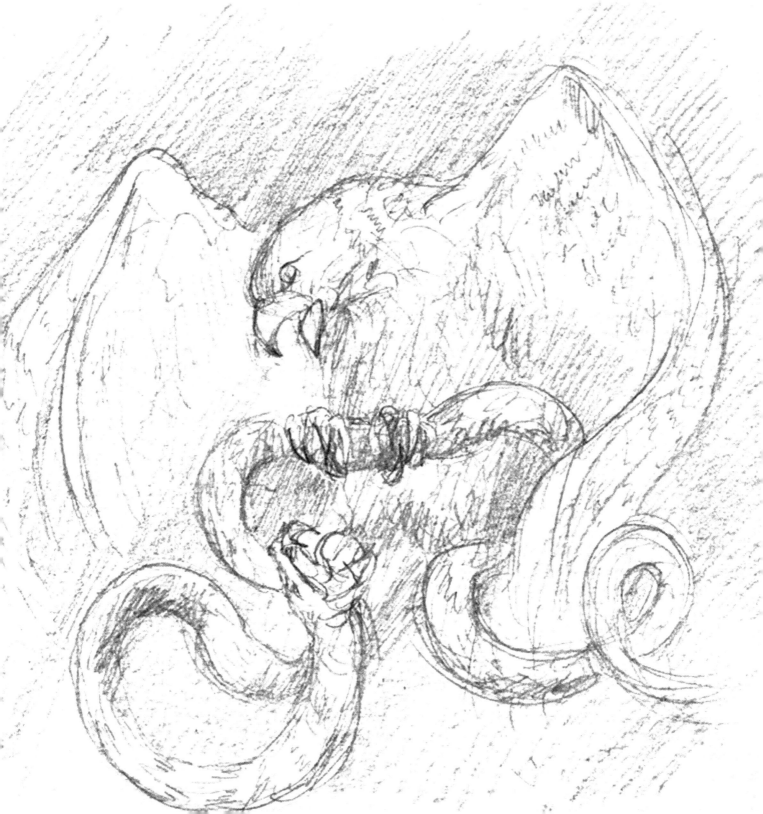

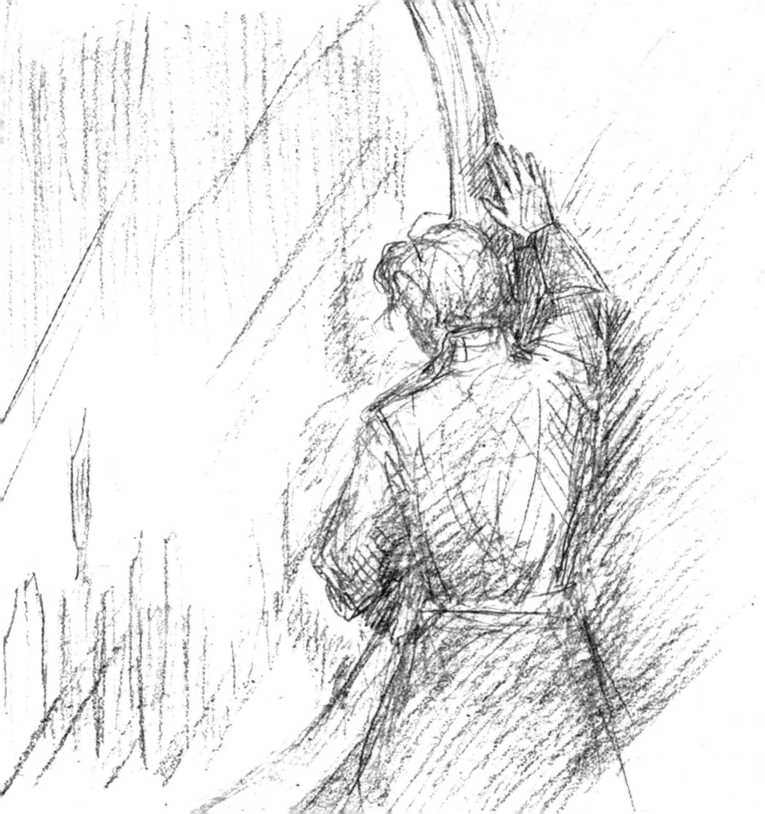

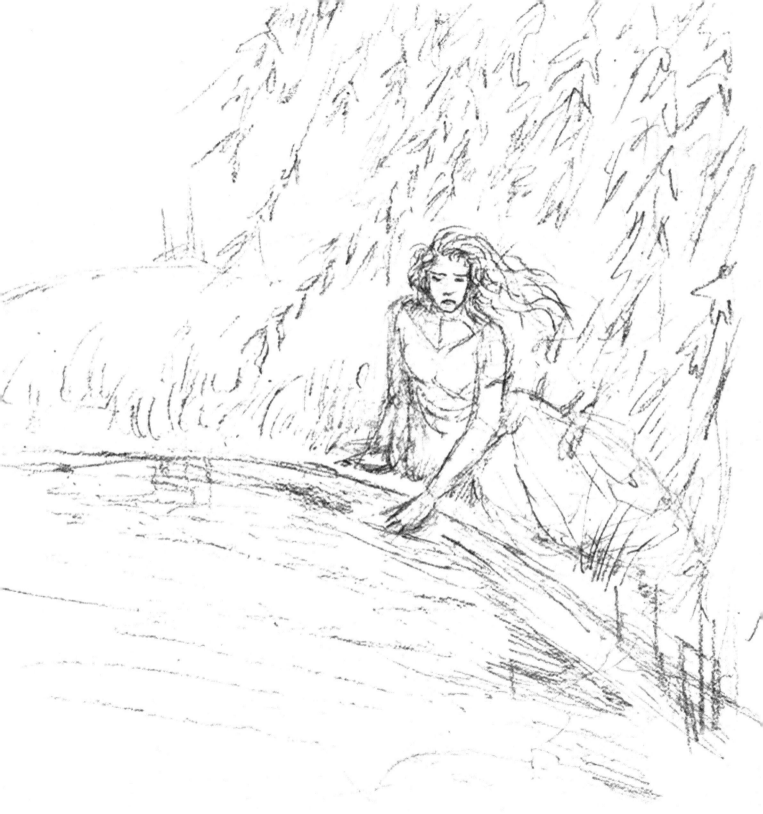

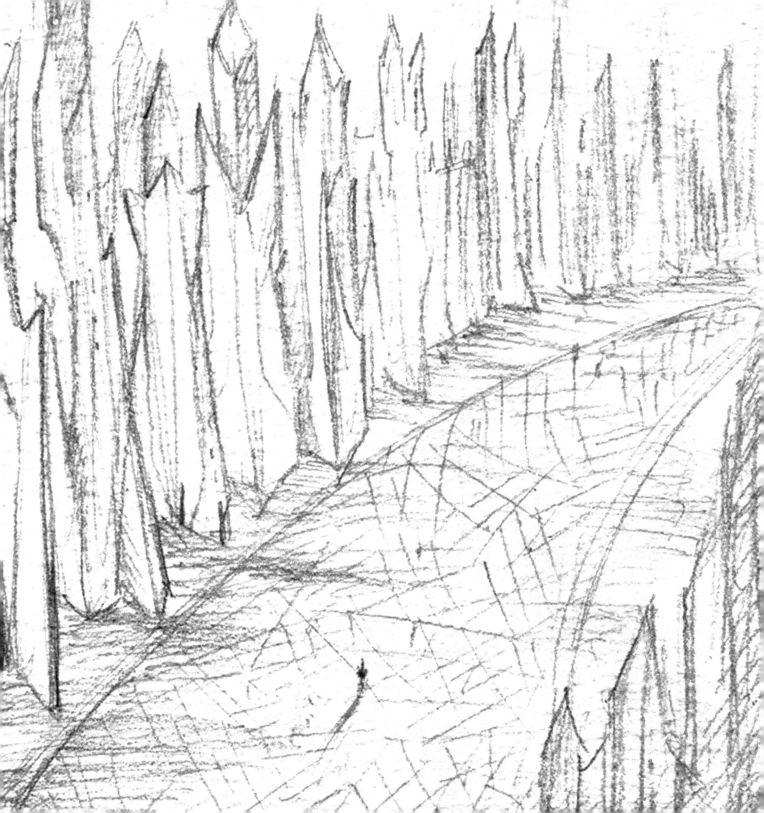

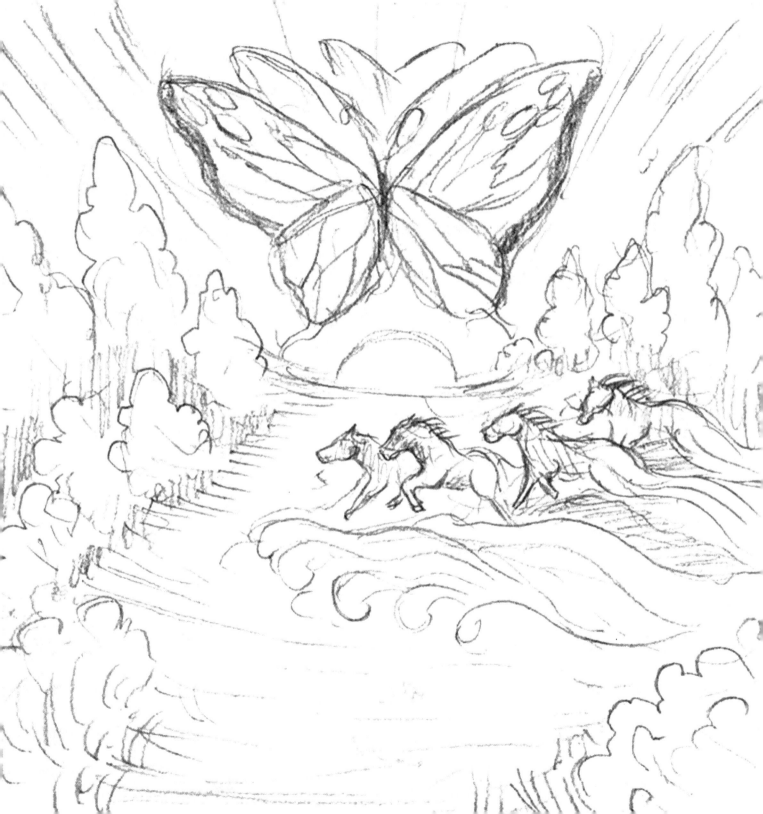

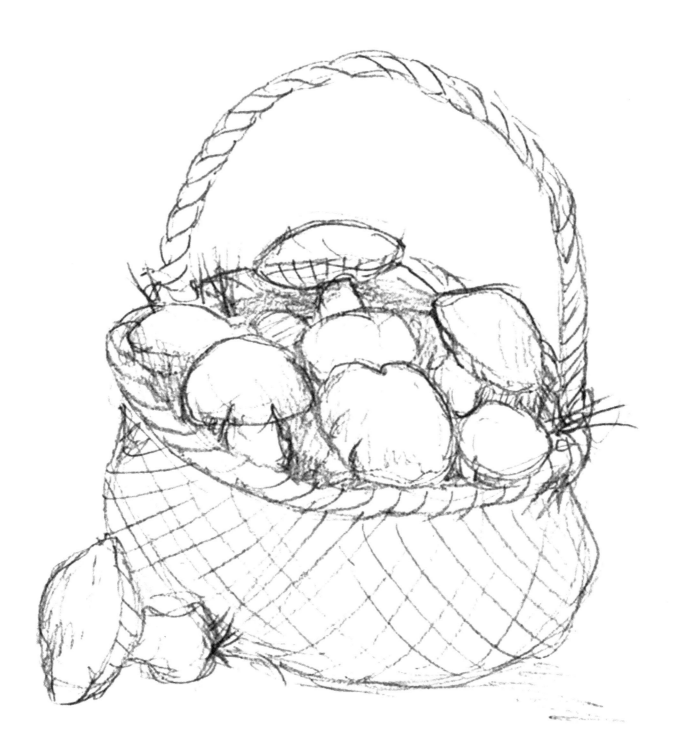

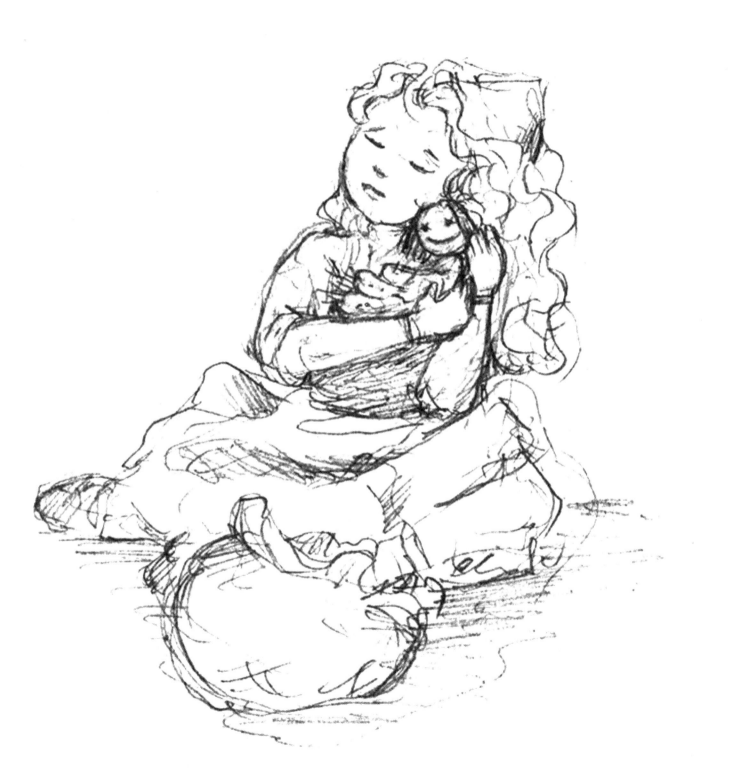

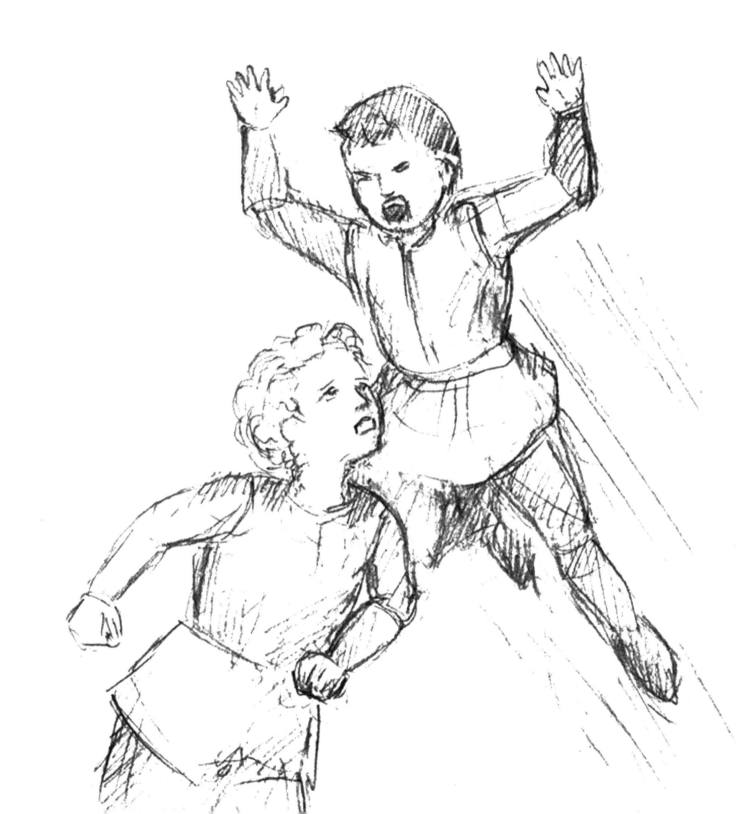

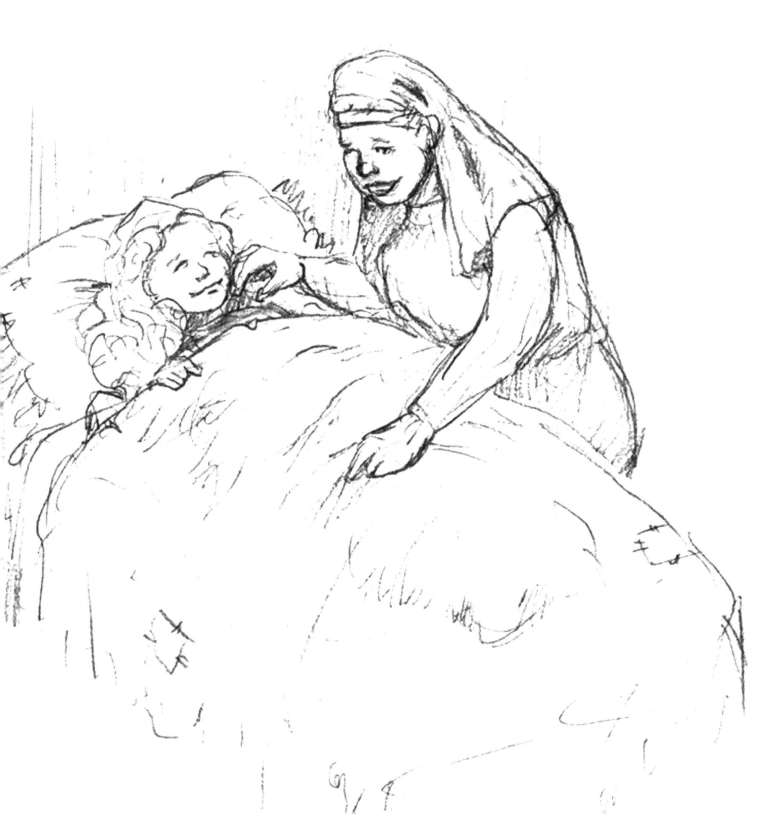

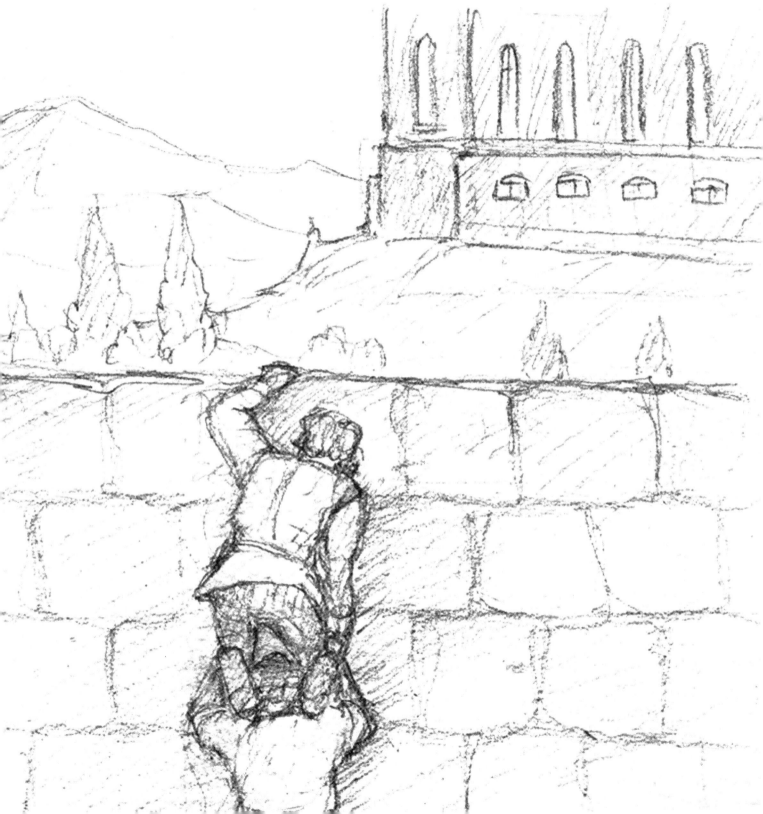

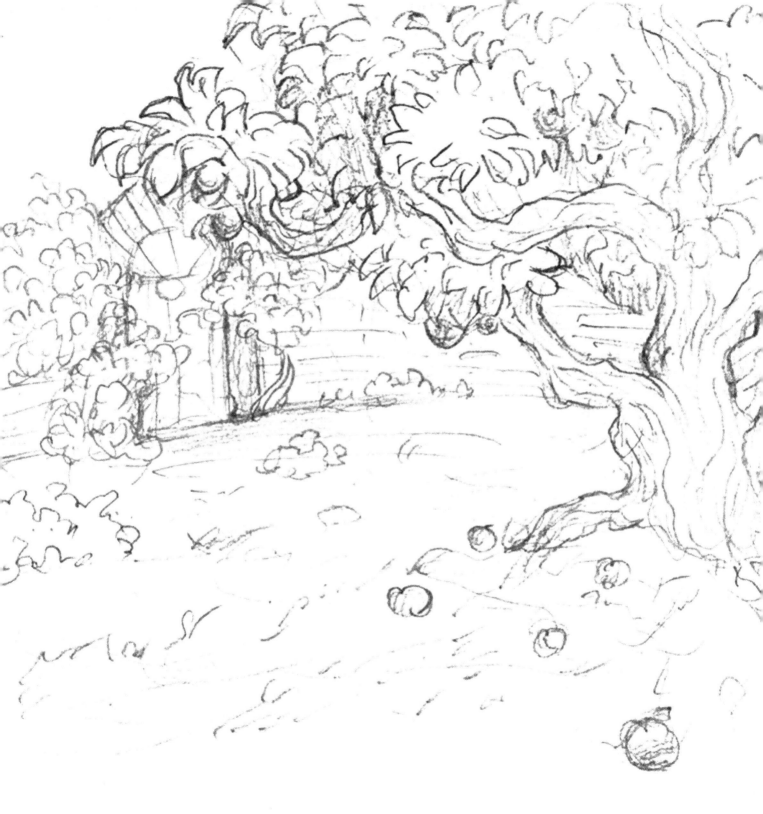

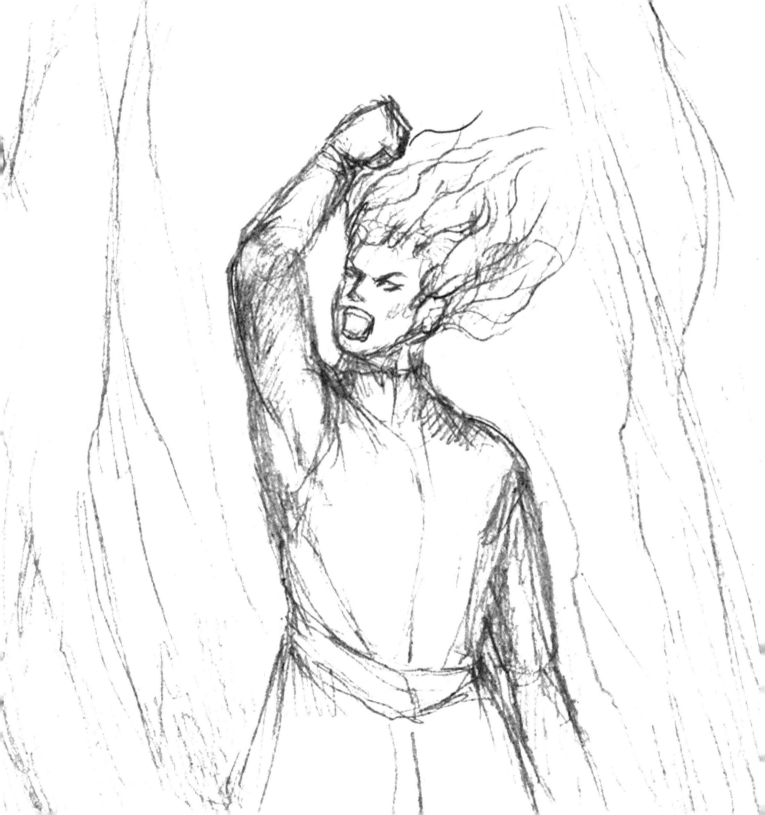

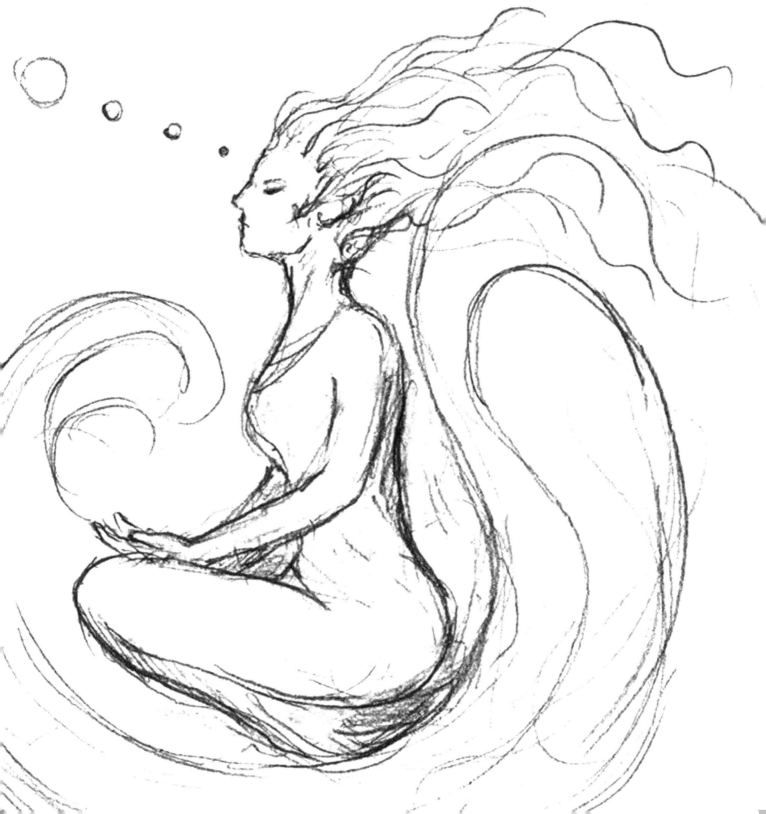

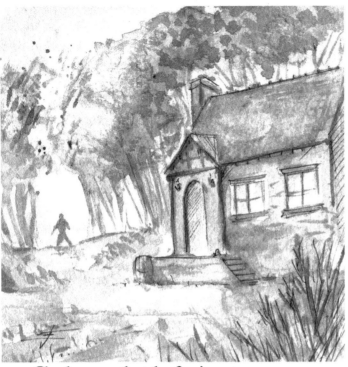

Charles sees that the fire is out

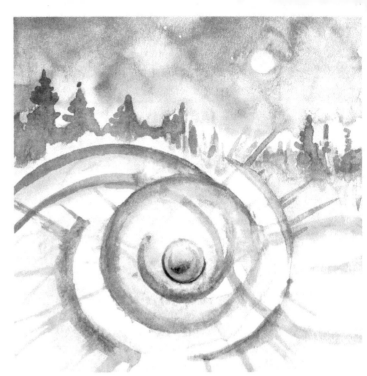

Charles sees a strange little moon outside the window

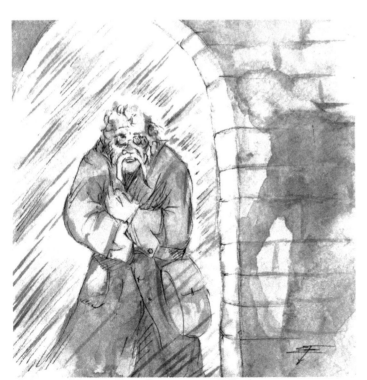

Master Fretwell arrives to see Maria

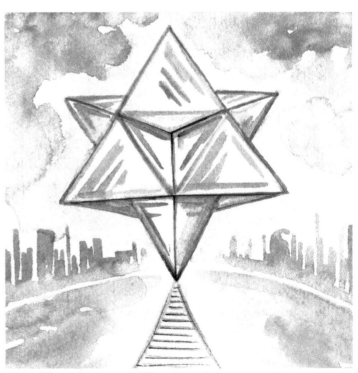

Tsera's world—The Apothese

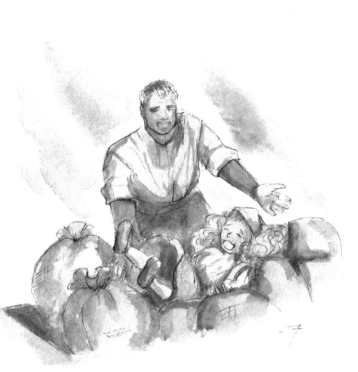

Charles throws Eleanor into the cart

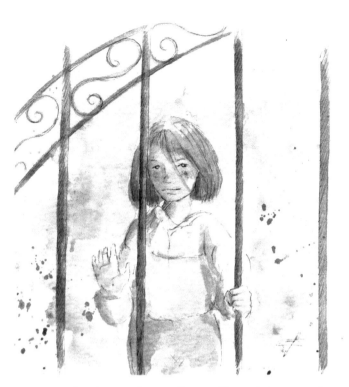

Audrey stares from the abbey gates

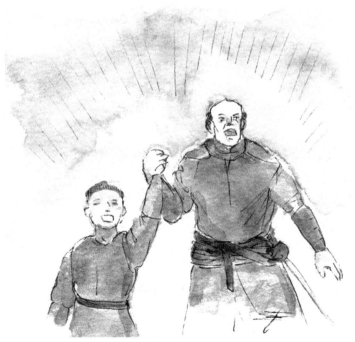

John wins the fencing match

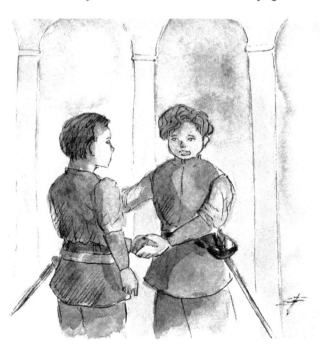

Edward congratulates John

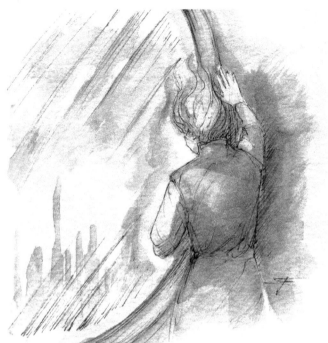

Lerion stares from Tsera's window

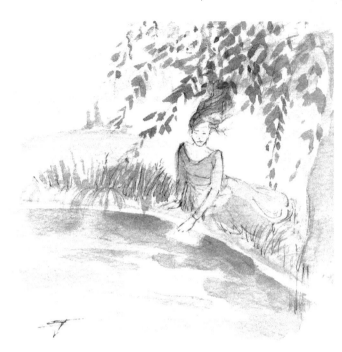

Lalycri sits by the lake

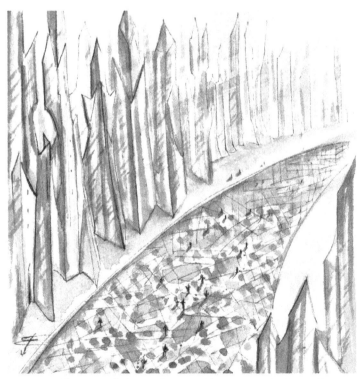

Lerion strides down the crystal path

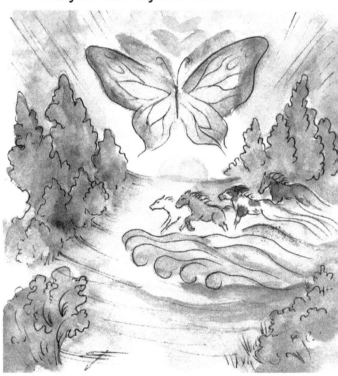

Inside Tsera's hologram

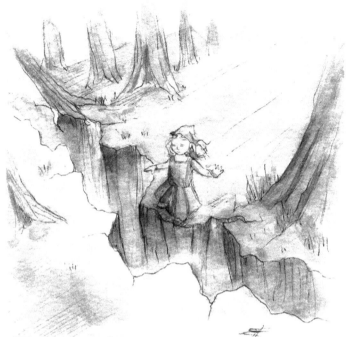

Eleanor stands at the edge of the fissure

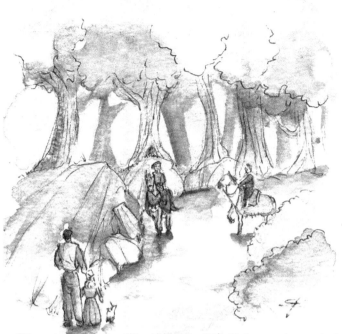

Charles finds Eleanor with Edward and John

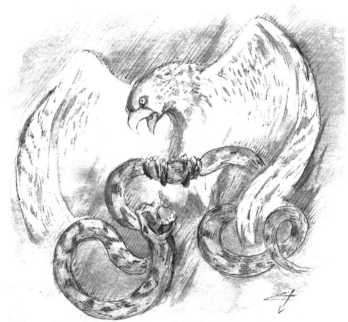

The white falcon saves Maria from the serpent

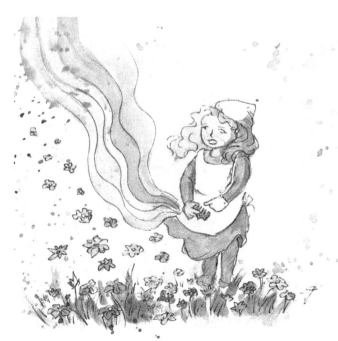

Eleanor uses the comb for the first time

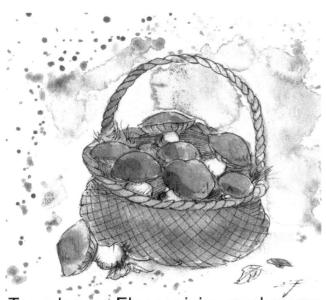

Tsera leaves Eleanor juicy mushrooms

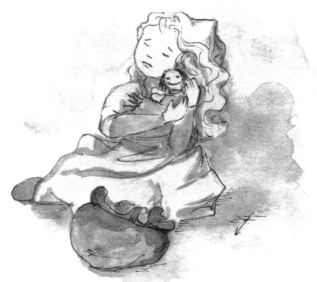

Charles must leave Eleanor at the abbey

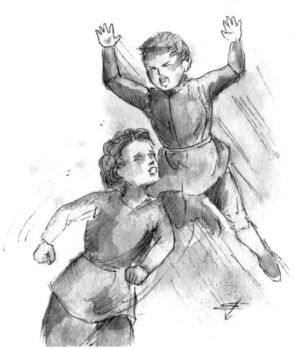

John and Edward fight over Eleanor

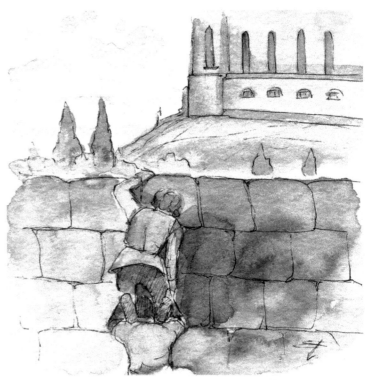

Edward and John find the walled garden

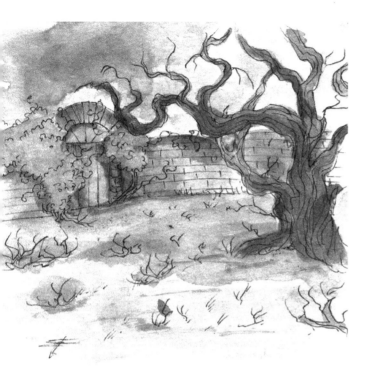

The land is dying

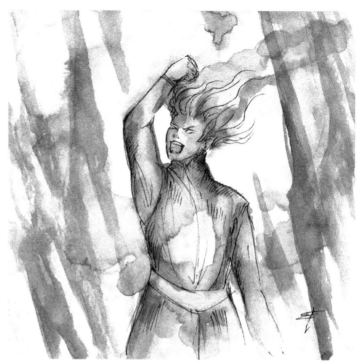

Lerion finds the second Vibration

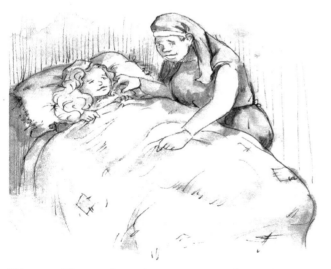

Sister Francis tries to comfort Eleanor

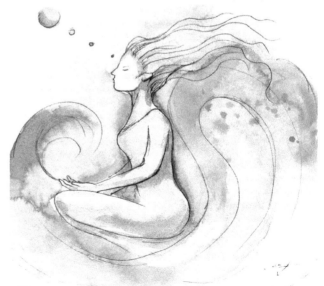

Tsera contemplates her experiment

9 781636 253718